SON OF SAM

THE BIOGRAPHY OF DAVID BERKOWITZ

PAUL BRODY

LifeCaps Biography Series
ANAHEIM, CALIFORNIA

Contents

About LifeCaps

LifeCaps is an imprint of BookCaps™ Study Guides. With each book, a lesser known or sometimes forgotten life is recapped.

We publish a wide array of topics (from baseball and music to literature and philosophy), so check our growing catalogue regularly (www.bookcaps.com) to see our newest books.

[1]

The Early Years of David Berkowitz

Betty Broder was a young, single parent struggling to get by in the Bedford-Stuyvesant neighborhood of Brooklyn, New York in the 1930s. Her family had pieced together a living during the Great Depression, and when Betty announced that she was getting married to Tony Falco, they had no money to help the young couple--even if they had approved of the marriage. The Broders were Jewish and were opposed to Betty marrying Falco, an Italian gentile. Betty and Tony managed to find money to open a fish market in 1939 before Betty gave birth to their only child, Roslyn. Sometime after Roslyn was born, Tony left Betty for another woman. Betty was forced to close the fish market and raise Roslyn on her own.

After getting involved with a married real estate agent named Joseph Kleinman, Betty became pregnant with his baby. Kleinman insisted that she could not keep the child, so she made arrangements to have the baby adopted. When the baby boy was born on June 1, 1953, Betty listed Tony Falco as the father on the child's birth certificate. Betty continued her relationship with Kleinman until his death in 1965 while the infant Richard David Falco went to live his life in the Bronx as the only child of Nathan and Pearl Berkowitz.

Nathan owned a hardware store and was frequently away from home. While there was tension between David and his father, who phrased David's presence in the world as "a mistake," he had an unusually close relationship to Pearl. Even she had a difficult time managing David, though. He was hyperactive, at times, and had a bully's streak in him. He was also bigger and heavier than other children his age, which made him feel like something of an outcast, even though neighbors remarked that he was a good-looking boy. David missed a terrific deal of school, possibly because of the teasing or possibly simply due to disinterest.

Despite these issues, there were certainly no signs of the magnitude of terror that David would inflict on the city of New York. When he was 7 years old, David was hit by a car and suffered a head injury, although it is not known if that had any long-term effects. However, David had a fetish for burning bugs, and that progressed to arson when he was older. Many that evaluated David as an adult believe that the loss of his mother also had an impact on him. When he was young, Nathan and Pearl did not tell their son that Pearl had already battled breast cancer once before. In 1965 and in 1967 the cancer returned, and David's world was turned upside down. He was shocked. He had no healthy method of coping with his mother's illness and watching her decline during her chemotherapy treatment. Predictably, when Pearl died in 1967, David was devastated.

David became increasingly introverted following his mother's death. He questioned whether it was part of God's larger plan to destroy him. His focus on his schoolwork at Christopher Columbus High School deteriorated along with his mental stability. In 1971, David was left alone in New York City when Nathan remarried a woman that David did not like. She did care for David much, either. Soon after the wedding, Nathan and his new wife moved to Boynton Beach near Miami, Florida. With no family and few friends, the environment was ripe for David to sink further and further into his fantasy world. His only real friend was a woman named Iris Gerhard, who David considered a girlfriend, although she saw their relationship as purely platonic. David joined the United States Army in the summer of 1971. The U.S. was involved in the Vietnam War at this time, but David avoided serving in Vietnam when he was assigned to a unit in Korea. Friends say that the Army changed him. His stint in the military not only provided him with his first sexual experience, which resulted in a sexually transmitted disease, but it also taught him to shoot a gun. He proved to be a good marksman. After he was honorably discharged from the Army in 1974, David returned to New York, with few prospects and no goals.

Berkowitz's Mental Decline

At 21 years old, Berkowitz was lonely when he returned to New York. Many of his friends had moved away and with no family to turn to, he used money he had saved to rent an apartment and enroll in classes at Bronx Community College. The friends that remained said that he returned from his service in the Army a devilishly difficult man to talk to and highly argumentative. His political views and his views on war changed, too. Berkowitz had been pro-military action when he joined the Army, but by the time he got out, he was more of a "dove," or a pacifist. A friend who spoke to reporters after Berkowitz's arrest in 1977 said that he thought that Berkowitz's "mind sort of went" while he was in the Army.

Berkowitz worked odd jobs, including spending time as a cab driver, a security guard, and finally as a mail sorter at the Bronx Post

Office, where he worked the night shift. His fellow postal worker employees described him as quiet, reserved, and shy, recalling that he rarely interacted with anyone unless he was spoken to first. Berkowitz rented an apartment for $250 a month in Yonkers. His neighbors thought that he was quick-tempered, and he became known to the local police department because of disputes with his neighbors. One of his neighbors was Craig Glassman, a corporal for the Westchester County Sheriff's Emergency Force. Glassman lived on the floor below Berkowitz and over time received four handwritten threatening notes. Edna Williams, who lived next door to Berkowitz, never saw him in the two years that they were neighbors.

At one point, Berkowitz reconnected with his birth mother, Betty Falco. He visited Betty and Roslyn regularly at first, but when he found out why he was given up for adoption, he lost interest in those relationships and stopped visiting. Those who have analyzed Berkowitz's past suggest that this disappointment, along with the death of his mother and his lack of success in developing successful relationships with women all combined to create a level of hatred for women that became deadly. When Berkowitz was in prison, he eventually admitted that this was, indeed, the real driving force behind his attacks despite his initial claims that he was driven by demons. In a letter to his father in late 1975, Berkowitz wrote about his depression and dark mood, saying, "The girls call me ugly and they bother me the most."

Before Berkowitz turned to murder, his infatuation was with fire. His pyromania resulted in him setting nearly 1,500 fires in New York City between 1974 and 1977. Each fire was carefully noted in a journal, in which he referred to himself as "The Phantom of the Bronx." FBI Agent Robert K. Ressler is noted for profiling the motivation and behavior of serial killers and interviewed Berkowitz in 1979. Regarding the subject of Berkowitz's pyromania Ressler said, "Most arsonists like the feeling that they are responsible for the excitement and violence of a fire. With the simple act of lighting matches, they control events in society that are not normally controlled..." As it was for many killers, Berkowitz felt that the fires gave him some sense of control when he felt like he could control darned little else in his life.

In 1975, Berkowitz met some men at a party who were interested in the occult. Berkowitz had a fascination with horror film, such as "Rosemary's Baby," and gravitated toward learning more about satanic rituals and the occult. He read the satanic bible, written by Anton LaVey, who founded the Church of Satan in the Bay Area. Berkowitz slowly sunk into a life that he was convinced was possessed by evil demons.

[2]
The Attacks Begin

Berkowitz's reign of terror on New York City began on Christmas Eve in 1975, about a month after he wrote to Nathan Berkowitz. He told his father, "It's cold and gloomy here in New York, but that's okay because the weather fits my mood — gloomy. Dad, the world is getting dark now."

That night Berkowitz took a large hunting knife onto the streets, looking for his first victim. When he saw a woman leaving a grocery store, he reportedly stabbed her several times. Berkowitz said that she simply turned to look at him and then ran away. The identity of the woman was never confirmed. However, that same night, he stabbed 15 year-old Michelle Forman six times. She screamed and fought Berkowitz off before she managed to get into a nearby apartment building for help. Forman survived the attack.

A month after the stabbings, Berkowitz moved out of his Bronx apartment and into a rental house in Yonkers. His landlords, Jack and Nann Cassara, owned a German shepherd that barked and howled incessantly. Later, Berkowitz would claim that the dog was possessed by demons that ordered him to kill young women. He said that when he returned home from working the night shift as a security guard that the barking and howling nearly drove him to suicide. Berkowitz said Jack Cassara was Captain Jack Cosmo, the leader of devil dogs that roamed the streets.

Berkowitz moved out of the Cassara house after three months, never returning for his security deposit. He then moved to an apartment at 35 Pine Street in Yonkers, but he didn't escape howling dogs. His new neighbor, Sam Carr, had a black Labrador retriever named Harvey, which Berkowitz first tried to kill with a

Molotov cocktail but then he simply shot him. Berkowitz later claimed that Sam Carr was possessed by demons and possibly by Satan. He said that the Son of Sam was the son of the demon that possessed Carr.

In May 1976, Berkowitz drove to Florida to visit his father in Boynton Beach. After that, he headed west to Houston, Texas to visit an Army buddy, Billy Dan Parker. A month later, as he was preparing to go back to New York, Berkowitz told Parker that he felt a little vulnerable driving all that way without some sort of protection. Berkowitz asked Parker if he would buy a gun for him, and Parker did not hesitate, later referring to Berkowitz as his best friend and saying it did not occur to him to say no.

On June 12, Berkowitz and Parker walked into Spring Branch Jewelry and Loan Pawn Shop. They walked out with a Charter Arms Bulldog .44 caliber revolver and three boxes of ammunition. It is a heavy gun and can be difficult to control for inexperienced shooters. The Bulldog was the final piece of the puzzle to the arsenal that Berkowitz had been putting together over the past several months. He already owned a Commando Mark III rifle, purchased in Brooklyn days after his permit was approved, a Glenfield rifle with a 4x14 telescopic sight, a Charter Arms AR-7 Explorer shotgun, and a 12-gauge Ithaca Deerslayer shotgun.

Berkowitz quit his job as a security guard on July 28 and took work as a cab driver with the Co-Op City Taxi Company. He learned the city streets as he drove, and when his shift was over, he returned to his apartment to eat or listen to records by his favorite singers, primarily Carole King, James Taylor, or Peter, Paul and Mary. On the nights he had insomnia, which was often, he listened to the same records over and over again. When he quit his job at the taxi company on July 19, nobody could even remember that he had worked there.

Berkowitz later said that his demons told him it was necessary to have a steady job, so he looked for work by day and victims by night. His Uncle Sol got him a job installing air conditioning ducts. He tried to be as "normal" as possible, but still kept to himself. Each night he checked his Charter Bulldog revolver to make sure it was still loaded, even though he had never removed the ammunition. When he left in the evening in search of victims, he went down the fire escape instead of the elevator, trying to avoid being noticed.

Donna Lauria and Jody Valenti

Around 1 a.m. on July 28, an 18 year-old brunette named Donna Lauria sat in a car that was parked in front of her apartment building in the Bronx. Lauria was an emergency medical technician and more mature than her years. Two days earlier her Uncle Ralph had died, and family that gathered in the wake of his passing remarked how beautiful Donna had become. A friend, Jody Valenti, sat with her in Donna's blue Oldsmobile Cutlass and the two girls were talking when Donna's parents, Mike and Rose, arrived home.

Mike stopped by the car and told his daughter that she needed to come up to the apartment soon. He had not been in the apartment for a minute when he heard shots. Berkowitz, dressed in jeans and a denim jacket, had approached the passenger side of the car, taken the .44 caliber Bulldog handgun from a paper bag, and squatted into a firing position. It took both hands for Berkowitz to control the kickback from the revolver. He fired through the passenger window five times. He continued to pull the trigger even after the chambers were empty.

Donna Lauria lay dying in a pool of blood from a neck wound as her father rushed toward the car. The 19 year-old Valenti cried hysterically as she inadvertently hit the car horn. Valenti survived the attack, suffering a leg wound from a shot to the thigh, and was able to provide police with a description of the shooter. Berkowitz drove away, unsure if the girls were alive or dead but happy that he had launched his first attack. In a city like New York, the murder barely caused a ripple in the news reports.

Carl Denaro and Rosemary Keenan

On October 23, 1976, Berkowitz climbed into his cream colored Ford and made his way to Queens. As he cruised the Flushing neighborhood, he noticed two people in a red Ford Galaxie. One of the people had long dark hair, his favorite, although he was not sure if the passengers in the car were male or female. He followed the red car to the corner of 33rd Avenue and 159th Street. When the red car parked, Berkowitz pulled his car in behind them.

Twenty year-old Carl Denaro, who was due to enter the Air Force, was on a date with 18 year-old Rosemary Keenan. He knew Keenan from college, and she was at the wheel after they left a party. Keenan was the daughter of a policeman with the New York City Police Department.

As Denaro and Keenan sat in the car, Berkowitz went to the passenger side window, pulled his .44 caliber gun from under his denim jacket, and fired five shots into the car window. As glass fragments flew, Keenan bolted from the car, unhurt. Denaro was struck in the head by a bullet. When Berkowitz left, Keenan got back into the car and drove Denaro to the hospital. He miraculously survived the shooting, although he did require a metal plate in his head where part of his skull had been blown away.

Donna DeMasi and Joanne Lomino

Donna DeMasi, 16 years of age, and Joanne Lomino, 18, had ventured into Manhattan on the cold and windy night of November 26, 1976 to see a movie. The girls took a bus to 262nd Avenue and Hillside and, around midnight, they started their walk to Joanne's house.

They noticed a dark-haired man following them and started to walk faster. Thinking that he was gone, they stood on the stoop of Joanne's house while she rummaged for her keys in her purse.

They both saw Berkowitz approach, although neither thought he seemed terribly menacing until his .44 caliber handgun was firing at them. Joanne's parents came out to find both girls shot. A bullet had gone through and exited DeMasi's body. Lomino was unable to move. Both DeMasi and Lomino survived, but Lomino was paralyzed from the waist down when a bullet severed her spine.

Christine Freund and John Diel

Shortly after midnight on January 30, 1977, Christine Freund and John Diel left the Wine Gallery in Queens, where they had enjoyed a late dinner after seeing the movie "Rocky" at the Continental Theater. Freund was 26 years old and worked on Wall Street. She had been dating 30 year-old Diel for seven years, and they were engaged to be married.

They made the short walk in the bitterly cold night to Diel's car and waited briefly for it to warm up after Diel started the engine. Suddenly, there was a large boom and glass exploded. Berkowitz had shot Freund in the head and chest.

She slumped in her seat as Diel, who was not hit, frantically tried to wave down passing cars for help. Meanwhile, someone had called the police after hearing gunshots and an ambulance arrived within minutes. Freund, who had come to the U.S. from Austria, was transported to St. John's Hospital, but she died later that morning.

Virginia Voskerichian

Virginia Voskerichian was also an immigrant. The 20 year-old junior at Columbia University was from Bulgaria. As she left the Forest Hills subway station on March 8, 1977, Berkowitz began to follow her. When he was within 25 feet, he took out his gun.

Instinctively, Voskerichian put her book up as a shield, but one of the shots that Berkowitz fired ripped through the book and made its way into her head. She fell into a row of pine bushes that lined the sidewalk. Voskerichian died at the same hospital where Freund had died a month earlier. Eyewitnesses gave police a description of the shooter, saying he was about 5 feet, 10 inches tall with dark, slicked-back hair.

Valentina Suriani and Alexander Esau

About midnight on April 17, 1977, 20 year-old Alexander Esau had taken Valentina Suriani to a late movie. Around 3 a.m., they were parked in a car along Hutchinson River Parkway, about three blocks from where Donna Lauria had been murdered. Berkowitz fired into the car four times. Esau and Suriani were both hit twice. A neighbor called the police, and when they arrived on the scene, they found Suriani dead behind the wheel and Esau critically wounded. Esau had been shot in the head, but he survived.

Police also found a letter at the scene, addressed to Captain Joseph Borelli, the head of Operation Omega, the task force charged with solving the Berkowitz murders. Operation Omega included Detective Redmond Keenan, the father of Rosemary Kennan. The letter was full of spelling errors and looked as if a child might have written it. Part of the letter said:

I am deeply hurt by your calling me a weman-hater. I am not. But I am a monster. I am the "son of Sam"...I feel like an outsider. I am on a different wavelength then everybody else - programmed to kill. However, to stop me you must kill me... I am the "monster" - "Beelzebub" - the chubby behemouth. I love to hunt. Prowling the streets looking for fair game - tasty meat. The wemon of Queens are prettiest of all... Mr. Borelli, sir, I don't want to kill any more. No sur, no more but I must, "honour thy father"...

Judy Placido and Sal Lupu

As the summer of 1977 heated up with panic over the murderer now called the Son of Sam, Berkowitz struck again on June 26, 1977. Even though the attacks had thinned out the crowds at the discos, Judy Placido and her date, Sal Lupo, were at the Elephas in Queens.

Placido was only 17, so perhaps she had used fake identification to get into the disco.

As they sat in a car around 3 a.m., Judy told Sal, "This Son of Sam is really scary. The way that guy comes out of nowhere. You never know where he'll hit next." And with that, there was a loud echo in the car that made Placido's ears ring. Lupo, who was not shot, ran back toward the club to get help, but when Placido tried to follow him, she collapsed. Placido was covered in blood from three gunshot wounds. Despite being shot three times, Placido survived and was not seriously injured, although scars from the wounds remained for years to come.

Bobby Violante and Stacy Moskowitz

On July 31, 1977, 20 year-old Bobby Violante had his first date with a pretty blonde named Stacy Moskowitz, also 20 years old. Violante, who had just started a career as a model, had met Moskowitz at "Gong Show Night" at a restaurant in Sheepshead Bay a few days before. Violante's mother warned him about the Son of Sam, who was still on the loose, but Violante told her she had nothing to worry about because Moskowitz was blonde.

They went to a movie before taking a drive along the water on Shore Parkway in Brooklyn. Berkowitz had not struck in Brooklyn, so Violante felt safe there and talked Moskowitz into taking a walk through the park. Violante later said they saw Berkowitz standing casually in the park, never imagining that he was the Son of Sam.

When they got back to Violante's car, Berkowitz fired into the passenger window. Violante thought he was dead, at first, but when he realized he was still alive, he managed to get out of the car before collapsing.

Moskowitz had been shot one time in the head. Meanwhile, Berkowitz calmly walked away from the scene while others rushed to the aid of Violante and Moskowitz.

Violante survived but lost all of the vision in his left eye and most of the vision in his right eye. Moskowitz died two days after the attack.

Stacy Moskowitz would be Berkowitz's final victim.

[3]

The Hunt for the Son of Sam

It took some time before the NYPD connected the crimes, primarily because there was little evidence to suggest that they were related in any way. This was in the days before computer databases could store valuable information that detectives in the 21st century rely on to help solve crimes. If the Son of Sam were to strike now, it is highly possible that something as basic as a fingerprint match would help police solve the case faster. However, in 1977, it was not until Voskerichians's death that the realization that a serial killer was on the loose descended on the city.

Investigators conclusively linked the deaths of Lauria and Voskerichian after determining that the same gun had been used to kill both young women. On March 10, NYPD Commissioner Michael Dodd held a press conference and announced the findings and a panic set over the city. Bars and discos lost business as young people were too afraid to be out at night. Berkowitz's tendency to choose brunette victims sent young women to the salon to dye their hair or to shops to buy blonde wigs.

Once the media realized that a serial killer was at large, news, and rampant speculation about the Son of Sam filled the newspapers and airwaves. The media frenzy was further fueled when one of the media's own became directly involved in the mystery. Author and investigative reporter Jimmy Breslin was one of the most popular newspaper columnists in New York in the 1970s. He had such influence that in 1970, he was attacked at a restaurant called The Suite, owned by mobster Henry Hill. Hill was a member of the Lucchese crime family.

Mafia man Jimmy Burke did not like a column Breslin had written about another member of the Lucchese crime family, Paul Vario, and ordered the hit on the writer. Breslin came away from the attack with a bloody nose and a concussion.

Breslin was writing for the New York Daily News when he received a letter on May 30, 1977. It was sent to his house, and his assistant, Ann Marie Caggiano, was the first to see it. She called Breslin and told him that he had received a "creepy" letter. The author of the handwritten letter said that he was the Son of Sam. The postmark on the front of the envelope indicated that it had been mailed earlier that same day from Englewood, New Jersey. On the back of the envelope were the neatly printed words: "Blood and Family – Darkness and Death – Absolute Depravity – .44" The letter began:

"Hello from the gutters of N.Y.C. which are filled with dog manure, vomit, stale wine, urine and blood. Hello from the sewers of N.Y.C. which swallow up these delicacies when they are washed away by the sweeper trucks. Hello from the cracks in the sidewalks of N.Y.C. and from the ants that dwell in these cracks and feed in the dried blood of the dead that has settled into the cracks. J.B., I'm just dropping you a line to let you know that I appreciate your interest in those recent and horrendous .44 killings. I also want to tell you that I read your column daily and I find it quite informative. Tell me Jim, what will you have for July twenty-ninth?"

The reference to the 29th of July was noting the first anniversary of the death of Donna Lauria. New York police were convinced that the Son of Sam was going to attack again on July 29. That did not happen, but Moskowitz and Violante were attacked two days later. Berkowitz came up with the idea of writing to Breslin after reading about a letter Jack the Ripper wrote in 1888. In the midst of a series of unsolved murders in London, volunteers formed The Whitechapel Vigilance Committee. George Lusk, the head of the committee, received a letter on October 16, 1888 that many believed was from the notorious serial killer. The letter was shipped to Lusk in a box that also contained part of a human kidney.

After reading the letter from Berkowitz, Breslin contacted the police, who noted that it differed in appearance dramatically from the letter left for Captain Borelli at the Suriani/Esau attack. Its neat appearance, along with the logos and symbols underneath the Son of Sam's signature, suggested that the letter may have been printed professionally or done by a calligrapher. However, some of the details also suggested that the person who wrote the letter knew facts about the crimes that the general public did not. With the permission of the police department, the Daily News printed part of the letter a week later, along with Breslin's column, urging the killer to turn himself in. That edition of the paper sold over a million copies and the panic in New York City intensified. Breslin, out of concern that the Son of Sam might be stalking him, sent his wife and daughter to stay out on Long Island until the killer was caught.

Operation Omega

Operation Omega was officially formed on April 14, 1977, nine months after the death of Donna Lauria. In the largest task force ever commissioned by the NYPD, Deputy Inspector Timothy J. Dowd led a team that would eventually include over 300 detectives. The cost to the city was over $90,000 a day. The department's best detectives were brought on board, and many of them spent the night on cots in the station house as they worked day and night in pursuit of the Son of Sam. However, as time went on, and the attacks continued, New Yorkers began to lose faith in their police department. Decades later, there is still criticism on how the police handled the evidence that was presented to them and the length of time it took to finally catch Berkowitz.

It was three days after Operation Omega was formed that Valentina Suriani and Alexander Esau were attacked. A team of 45 psychiatrists at Bellevue Hospital analyzed the letter that Berkowitz left at the scene for Captain Borelli and concluded that Berkowitz might be paranoid schizophrenic, possibly under the belief that he is possessed by the devil. The psychological profile they put together suggested that the killer they sought was a loner who had difficulty forming relationships, especially with women. When this information was released to the public, it unleashed a flood of tips, all determined to be worthless.

Carr in Yonkers

On June 10, 1977, Berkowitz's former landlord, Jack Cassara received a strange note in the mail from Yonkers. Included in the envelope was a photograph of a German shepherd. The brief note said:

"Dear Jack, I'm sorry to hear about that fall you took from the roof of your house. Just want to say 'I'm sorry' but I'm sure it won't be long until you feel much better, healthy, well and strong: Please be careful next time. Since your going to be confined for a long time, let us know if Nann needs anything.

Sincerely: Sam and Francis"

Cassara had not fallen off his roof, and he had no idea who Sam and Francis Carr were.

He looked their names up in the phonebook and called them to discuss the note. The Carrs did not know who the Cassaras were, either, and furthermore could not understand why someone would send a note to Jack Cassara, pretending to be them. The Carrs decided to get together with Jack Cassara and his son, Stephen, to talk about the note more in person.

When the Carrs and the Cassaras met, they looked at the letter and the photo. The Carrs told Jack that their small dog had been shot, and their neighbor's German shepherd had been shot, too. Stephen Cassara brought up the strange tenant, David Berkowitz, who rented a room in their house a year earlier and had a strong dislike for their dog. The Cassaras remembered him not just because of his problem with the dogs, but because he left so abruptly and never returned for his $200 security deposit. The Carrs realized that they were talking about the same person who complained about their barking dog when he was their neighbor. He was also the man that they strongly suspected of shooting their dog. They notified the police departments in Yonkers and New Rochelle. Nann Cassara is the person who put two and two together when the police eventually called her back two months later. She speculated that their strange tenant, David Berkowitz, might be the Son of Sam.

The police officer who responded from the Yonkers police department happened to remember Craig Glassman, the deputy sheriff who lived next door to Berkowitz who had received the odd letters from him. One of the letters was about a group of demons that included the Carrs, the Cassaras, and Glassman. It was a remarkable coincidence. The Yonkers police department checked for the address and car registration information on Berkowitz, discovering that a Ford Galaxie was registered to him and that his driver's license was suspended. And then the police did nothing further with the information. Two weeks later, Judy Placido and Sal Lupo were shot.

A month after the Placid and Lupo shootings, Stacy Moskowitz was killed and Bobby Violante was blinded. Police interviewed a witness, Cacilia Davis, who had been out walking her dog. She said that she saw a Volkswagen bus leaving the scene, as well as a man that she thought was trying to hide in the bushes, possibly while concealing a gun. Her description of the man seemed too far off of the profile they had of the Son of Sam, although wanted posters with a man matching her description soon flooded the city.

The officers put little credence into Davis's tory, but did decide to look into her adamant claim that there was a patrol officer in the neighborhood that night who was writing parking tickets. Davis said that she saw a man take a ticket off his car, toss it away in disgust, and speed away. It seemed obvious to Davis that this man was connected to the Moskowitz/Violante shooting. When the officers checked into her story, they discovered that a ticket had, indeed, been issued to David Berkowitz of 35 Pine Street in Yonkers, who drove a Ford Galaxie with license plate number 561-XLB. Detective James Justus from the 10th homicide zone tried to call Berkowitz many times, thinking he might be a witness to the shootings, but nobody ever answered the phone.

On August 9, Detective Justus called the Yonkers police department, still trying to get in touch with Berkowitz. The woman who answered the phone asked if the David Berkowitz Justus was looking for had ever lived at 35 Pine Street. Detective Justus was speaking with Sam Carr's daughter, Wheat. When Justus confirmed that Berkowitz's address was 35 Pine Street, Carr's daughter told him that Deputy Glassman had received threatening letters from Berkowitz. She also told Justus that he needed to speak to her father, who was frustrated at what he viewed as inaction by the police department on the information he had given them. Carr had, in fact, given them the name of the Son of Sam killer.

Justus did call Sam Carr, who recounted the story about the dog shooting and told him that Officers Chamberlain and Intervallo had more information. Chamberlain and Intervallo did debate about how much investigative work they should do on the Berkowitz lead. They did not want to appear to be stepping on the toes of the Omega detectives and disrupting the chain of command. They did go so far as to check into their computer database for a description of Berkowitz, based on the information provided on his driver's license. The description did match what they knew of the Son of Sam. When Justus called and spoke to Chamberlain, Chamberlain told him that Berkowitz did bear a strong resemblance to the police artist sketches.

Evidence pointing to Berkowitz began to pile up, in addition to the lead that Cacilia Davis had provided. Reports came that there was a suspected arson on Pine Street, where Berkowitz's apartment was located. When the police arrived, they spoke to Deputy Glassman. He showed the police .22 caliber bullets that had been placed near his door. Berkowitz had started a fire, which was quickly put it out, but it was obvious that he had intended to set the bullets off with the fire. Glassman also showed the police the letters he had received from Berkowitz, which were a match to the letter sent to Jack Cassara. Glassman, who died in a car accident in 1991, told his family repeatedly that the police ignored his information about Berkowitz for too long. He died believing that his role in capturing Son of Sam was unappreciated.

Meanwhile, Carr had grown tired of waiting for the Omega task force to act on his leads. He went to police headquarters to ask why he was being ignored, and he was told that he was one of many people who claimed to have information on the Son of Sam. Carr was sent away.

Ultimately, the evidence was too strong to deny that David Berkowitz should be considered a prime suspect as the Son of Sam. Detectives, including Ed Zigo, arrived at 35 Pine Street and spotted Berkowitz's Ford Galaxie. Zigo looked in the backseat of the car – without a search warrant – and discovered an Army duffel bag containing underwear, a toothbrush, and a rifle. Zigo looked in the glove compartment and found a handwritten letter that was addressed to the Suffolk County Police Department. The letter said that there was going to be an attack on a disco in the Hamptons.

Zigo was sent to get a search warrant while other detectives stayed behind. The scene began to draw a crowd of patrol officers and detectives while curious neighbors and passersby watched to see what would develop. A detective asked the driver of a passenger van to park as close to Berkowitz's Ford as he could, making it harder for Berkowitz to get away if he came out of his apartment. Berkowitz had yet to appear from his small apartment, which was strewn with pornographic magazines and had bizarre quotes scribbled on the walls. The apartment's windows were covered with dirty sheets.

Omega sent a SWAT team to form a perimeter around the building on Pine Street. The first person that the SWAT team mistakenly snared was Glassman. Finally, at 10:30 p.m. on August 10, 1977, Berkowitz emerged from the building. The police watched him as he walked. Dressed in jeans and a light blue button-down shirt, carrying a brown paper bag, he got into his car and started the engine. Detective John Falotico approached the car with his gun drawn. He tapped on the car window. Berkowitz looked up at Falotico and said, "You got me. How come it took you such a long time?"

[4]

THE ARREST OF DAVID BERKOWITZ

The next day, a picture of a grinning David Berkowitz was splashed across the front page of The New York Times. Below that was a close-up photo of the handgun believed to be the weapon used in the shootings that had terrorized the city for over a year.

Berkowitz had been briefly held at the Yonkers Police Department before being taken to police headquarters on Centre Street, where he was met by Mayor Abe Beame, who mistook him for a detective and tried to shake his hand. Predictably, the media swarmed the area around the police department. The arrest was headline news around the world. Roone Arledge, the head of ABC news, arrived and personally directed his staff using a walkie-talkie.

Mayor Beame spoke to the media at 1 a.m. and advised that police had captured the man they believed to be the Son of Sam. Many were surprised to see that the demon that had been haunting the streets of New York was a young, chubby, postal worker with creepy grin. The first detective to speak to Berkowitz after his arrest, Joe Coffey, said that talking to him was like "talking to a head of cabbage." Coffey said, "I walked into the conference room in a rage, but I would up feeling sorry for the guy." Calmly, Berkowitz recounted each attack in detail that only the shooter would know. Coffey was convinced that they had the Son of Sam.

On August 11, Berkowitz was charged with second-degree murder in the death of Stacy Moskowitz. Berkowitz said only "yes" to the judge when asked to confirm his identity. As a crowd gathered outside the courthouse yelling, "Kill! Kill!" Judge Richard Brown ordered a psychiatric evaluation to determine if Berkowitz was fit to stand trial. Nathan Berkowitz refused to respond to requests for interviews as he made his way to New York from Florida to see his son. One of Berkowitz's attorneys, Leon Stern, had to duck into a room in the courthouse for protection from a mob that mistakenly believed he was Berkowitz's father. An AP photo showed John Diel, working as a bartender at a New York club, having a celebratory drink in honor of the arrest.

The New York Post, owned by Rupert Murdoch, printed a sensational article titled "How I Became a Mass Killer," with Berkowitz listed as the author. The article featured a series of letters that he had supposedly written to an old girlfriend. Murdoch's paper also printed a large, grainy black and white photo of Berkowitz sleeping on a cot in the psychiatric ward at King's County Hospital with the caption, "Sam Sleeps." The role of the media had already come into question, as there was a widespread belief that Berkowitz had been transformed into a celebrity. In the August 15 issue of The New Yorker, which was published before Berkowitz was arrested, the argument was made that the fame that was being lavished on the Son of Sam might be pushing him to strike again.

Photos of Berkowitz's apartment – Apartment 7E – showed what was referred to as "Satan's Lair." The studio apartment overlooking the Hudson River had few of Berkowitz's personal possessions, other than a scrapbook that he kept of his exploits. He had a mattress with no bed frame on a shag rug and various books and pamphlets. Photos show holes in the wall with notes written on the wall saying that baby killers were inside. "Sam Carr – My Master" was written on the wall near his mattress. The apartment building still stands, although the address has changed to 42 Pine. It still attracts those who are curious about its notorious past.

Berkowitz followed the media coverage of his killings particularly closely, and his scrapbook was thick with numerous photos and newspaper clippings of his crimes. He was apparently especially a fan of the Post's coverage of him as he asked to read the post while he was in jail. Of course, that, too, became headline news for The Post. Jimmy Breslin said that he asked a police captain to get word to Berkowitz while he was still at King's County that he should write to Breslin and ask Breslin to say something good about him. Breslin said that Berkowitz was so medicated that he simply threw away the letter that Berkowitz sent, saying, "We can't make a living with that. I need the real thing!" Certainly, the idea that a jury might be swayed by what is printed in the press is always a concern, but Thomas Powers wrote in Commonweal in September 1977 that "Criticizing the tabloids for their all-out pursuit of Sam is a bit like criticizing the lion for gorging on the lamb. It neglects the nature of the beast."

The media frenzy around Berkowitz's arrest sparked a new set of laws in New York called the Son of Sam laws. The laws were enacted after rumors that publishers were in a bidding war to publish the Son of Sam's story. The law permitted the state of New York to take any money that criminals earned from deals like this for five years. The money the state seized was to go to compensation for victims. However, the Supreme Court struck down the laws in

1991. In 2006, Berkowitz settled a lawsuit against his former attorney, Mark Jay Heller, who Berkowitz accused of stealing his personal photos and letters. Heller wrote the self-published book "Dear David" and Berkowitz said that Heller was using the property that he entrusted to Heller in order profit for his own gain. Berkowitz said that he would drop the lawsuit if Heller gave the profits to the families of Berkowitz's victims. They eventually agreed to settle the suit when Heller turned over his profits to the state Crime Victims Fund.

Ultimately, concerns about a jury would be moot because there would be no trial. Berkowitz quickly confessed to the six murders. His attorneys entered an innocent plea for him days after his arrest and said they would use an insanity defense, but Berkowitz did not want to go trial. Years later he said, "I just wanted to end it, and I was just so distraught. I just confessed and pled guilty and got it over with, and -- just wanted to get out of that environment."

His sentencing was scheduled for June 10, 1978. Jimmy Breslin was there, as was Neysa Moskowitz, Stacy's mother. She had been part of a group of protestors outside of the King's County mental ward who did not like public dollars being spent on the evaluation of Berkowitz's mental capacity. "He is a bastard. I could kill him with my bare hands, and I am not a violent person. I could probably kill him and go for a dinner and go to sleep that night truly peacefully," Neysa Moskowitz said. Anton Arnold, Christina Freund's uncle, was also part of the group of protestors, and he said, "The quicker they destroy him, the better. The longer they keep him, the more it costs taxpayers' money."

The day of his sentencing, Neysa Moskowitz stood up in the courtroom and shouted at Berkowitz. Breslin recalled of Berkowitz, "He loved it." Berkowitz said calmly, over and over again, "Stacy is a whore." He did not shout it, but said it loud enough for everyone to hear." Breslin said, "He was nuts." Berkowitz then bolted for a window, knocking down nine or 10 guards in the process. "He had inhuman strength. You could see he was a dangerous man..." Breslin said. Sentencing was delayed because of the outburst, but State Supreme

Court Justice Joseph Corso said that Berkowitz would be sentenced on June 12, even if he had to be bound and gagged. On June 12, Berkowitz was sentenced to six consecutive life sentences in prison. The first time he would be eligible for parole was 2002. Breslin heard from Berkowitz one last time when he received a Christmas card that said, "Merry Christmas from the devil."

[5]
Prison Life

Berkowitz's first few years of prison life were problematic. He was a disciplinary problem and said that when he was first incarcerated, he was tormented by thoughts of suicide. He told Larry King of CNN in 1999, "I saw no hope in living. I was disgusted with my life. I was angry at a lot of people. I felt betrayed, confused, and I saw no hope." He also liked to torment other inmates. Perhaps as retaliation for Berkowitz's open discussion of his involvement with satanic cults, a fellow inmate at the Attica Correctional Facility attacked him with a homemade knife on July 10, 1979. A large gash opened up on Berkowitz's neck, although he managed to walk to the prison infirmary under his own power. He received 56 stitches.

Even with Berkowitz safely behind bars, the questions of why he committed these heinous crimes were still unanswered. Initially, he maintained the claim that he was part of a satanic cult and that he did not act alone. At one point, he said the song "Rich Girl" by Hall and Oates inspired him to kill. The story that he stuck with the most was that demons ordered him to kill. The idea that Berkowitz heard a dog commanding him to kill was certainly good for newspaper and magazine sales, even if it was not the truth.

Carl Denaro, one of the survivors of the Berkowitz attacks, said he thinks that Berkowitz did not act alone. He said that in the attack on him and Rosemary Keenan, there were five shots, but only three came from the same location. He also said that Berkowitz was too far away to shoot so accurately in the Lomino and DeMasi attack. Denaro also believed Berkowitz when he told Larry King in 1999 that he was part of a larger satanic cult, primarily because he thinks that Berkowitz seems like the type of man who would want to belong to something.

Among those that believed that David Berkowitz was faking mental illness and a belief in the occult was FBI Agent Robert Ressler. He met with Berkowitz three times in 1979 when Berkowitz was at Attica. Berkowitz told Ressler that he invented the story about being possessed by demons in case he needed an insanity defense if the police ever caught up to him. He told Ressler that the real reason he targeted the young women is because of resentment he harbored from being rejected by his adoptive mother. That he never had a true girlfriend and felt inadequate around women compounded his feelings.

Berkowitz also told Ressler that he wanted to attend the funerals of his victims, but he was afraid he would be discovered. He searched for the graves of his victims, but could not find them, and he hung around diners where the police liked to take coffee breaks to see if he could overhear any details about his crimes. He did return to the scene of the crimes when he could not find new victims, and so he could relive the attacks. Seeing chalked outlines and spots of blood staining the concrete was an erotic experience for him.

In the novel "Son of Sam," published in 1987, author Lawrence Klausner based his story on Berkowitz's claim that he was possessed by demons. He used Berkowitz's prison diaries as a resource and came away believing that Berkowitz lived in a fantasy world created by his psychosis. Three psychiatrists that evaluated Berkowitz in prison believed it, too. "All I had to do was slip 'Sam Carr' and the 'demons' into the conversation," Berkowitz said of one of the psychiatrists. "Why he would practically be wiping the tears from my eyes and comforting me. Goodness, what a nice man he was."

Dr. David Abrahamsen did not believe it, though, saying that Berkowitz invented the entire notion that he was insane. Berkowitz was taken by this view and began to write to Abrahamsen from his prison cell. They exchanged a series of letters in which Berkowitz would reflect on the shootings, as well as his life, answering questions that Abrahamsen posed to him. Abrahamsen came away from the experience believing that while Berkowitz was indeed a deeply troubled man, the root of his problems was the fact that he was given up for adoption, followed by the death of Pearl Berkowitz. Berkowitz told Abrahamsen that after his adoptive mother's death, "I lost the capacity to love."

Abrahamsen wrote "Confessions of Son of Sam" in 1985 and said that Berkowitz's feelings of abandonment were made worse after finding Betty Falco, his birth mother. Initially, the relationship was welcomed by both of them. Betty called him "Richie," since his given name at birth was Richard. When he visited her, Berkowitz played the role of "Richie the nice guy." Yet, as he discovered the circumstances of his birth and subsequent adoption, coupled with the fact that his half-sister Roslyn was not given up for adoption, Berkowitz became angry. He believed what Nathan had told him – that he was a mistake.

Over time, Berkowitz's rage grew and, as he told Abrahamsen, "I was getting a very powerful urge to kill most of my 'natural' family." Within a few months of these feelings developing, the killings, or as Abrahamsen phrased it, "the hunting," began. Berkowitz wrote that he had conflicting feelings about women, on one hand wanting to love them, but, on the other hand, wanting to destroy them. He especially disliked watching women dance, which could have been related to the fact that Betty was a former dancer. The sensuality that young women displayed while dancing seemed to cause even more conflicting emotions in Berkowitz. When he searched for young female victims in cars, especially those that might have been kissing their dates in the cars, Berkowitz saw Betty in those cars. When he shot the young women, he was shooting at an image of his birth mother in an amorous embrace with Kleinman, the married real estate agent who was his natural father. After the killings began, Berkowitz visited Betty and Roslyn for a while longer, his gun stowed in his car in case he "needed" it.

Eventually, Berkowitz grew unhappy with his relationship with Abrahamsen. He believed that the doctor was trying to fit Berkowitz in a mold that suited his own needs. When he no longer aligned with the interpretation of his personality as presented by Abrahamsen, Berkowitz latched on to a journalist, Maury Terry, who had started writing about the murders before Berkowitz was arrested. He said sarcastically of Abrahamsen, "Yeah, everything is the fault of the mother. Abrahamsen was so full of himself he got right to the brink of getting the truth, and he stopped."

Terry, a former business journalist for IBM, believes not only Berkowitz's claims that he was involved in Satanism, but that he was part of a larger satanic cult that was also responsible for the Charles Manson murders. Terry said that Berkowitz's belief in the occult was brought on not by insanity, but Berkowitz's intense loneliness. Like Carl Denaro, Terry believes that Berkowitz was susceptible to falling for anything that gave him a sense of belonging. He said that none other than Michael Carr, Sam Carr's son, introduced Berkowitz to Satanism. Berkowitz told him that one night he had a chance meeting with Michael outside of his apartment in Bronx. Michael invited him to attend a meeting at Untermeyer Park in Yonkers, which Terry said was the meeting place for the Westchester County branch of the Process Church of the Final Judgment. The church was part of a larger satanic network.

In 1987, Terry published the book "The Ultimate Evil," which attempts to show the link between the Charles Manson and Son of Sam murders. In it he said that a short time after Berkowitz began attending these meetings, he was pledging to Lucifer, also known as Samhain. This, Terry claims, is the source of the name Son of Sam, not Sam Carr, the owner of the possessed dog. The satanic cult that Berkowitz got involved with initially started setting fires and sacrificing animals before moving on to murder. Terry said that Berkowitz worked with this cult to carry about the Son of Sam attacks. Berkowitz reportedly told Terry that he was only responsible for three of the murders, but was present for all of the shootings.

Enough people believe that Berkowitz did not act alone in his attacks and that a cult was behind it all that the Yonkers police department reopened the Berkowitz case in 1996, but closed it again when no new evidence was uncovered. Still, there are questions that leave the door open to the possibility that Berkowitz did not act alone. None of the six police artist sketches of Berkowitz look like, and one of them actually bears a strong resemblance to Michael Carr. Berkowitz himself has said it enough times that a cult's involvement could be plausible. In a 1993 interview with Terry on the television show "Inside Edition," Berkowitz said, "The killings were another sacrifice to our gods, bunch of scumbags that they were." Later, he addressed the notion that he was part of cult when he said, "We made a pact, maybe with the devil, but also with each other...we were going to go all the way with this thing. We were soldiers of Satan now."

In another odd development, John Carr, Sam Carr's other son, was found dead at an Air Force Base in Minot, South Dakota six months after Berkowitz was arrested. His death was initially ruled a suicide, but authorities in South Dakota later speculated that it was a homicide. Henry Cinotti, a detective from the Bronx, faced disciplinary charges because he believed in the conspiracy theories and flew to South

Dakota to investigate John Carr's death. Michael Carr later died in a one-car auto accident when the car he was driving crashed into a pole. Autopsy results showed that he had a high blood-alcohol level, despite the fact that he was known not be a drinker. Berkowitz said that John and Michael were probably killed by the cult.

[6]

BERKOWITZ, THE BORN AGAIN CHRISTIAN

Ten years after he was incarcerated, 34 year-old Berkowitz was approached by another inmate named Rick. He talked to Berkowitz, who other inmates referred to as "Berserkowitz," about his anger. Rick told him that God had sent him to deliver the message that God loved and forgave him for his sins. Berkowitz was skeptical at first, saying that he was too evil for God's love. However, after spending some time talking to Rick, Berkowitz began to read the Bible. He thought the Psalms were especially beautiful. One night in 1987, as he read the Psalms in his prison cell, he said cried out to the Lord and asked for forgiveness for his sins.

As Berkowitz, the former Jew, delved deeper into Christianity, he took on a new identity. The mass murderer was now an evangelical Christian, and before long, Berkowitz was operating a letter-writing ministry from his prison cell at Sullivan Correctional Facility in Fallsburg, New York, 100 miles north of New York City.

He is considered by many evangelicals to be an apostle, similar to the modern-day Paul. A friend who is a former law enforcement officer said that Berkowitz is like Jesus and that being in prison, living a life stripped of modern conveniences, is actually an advantage for Berkowitz. "He is away from all the distractions," the friend said. To those that see Berkowitz this way, prison is like his cross, a symbol of suffering.

Berkowitz, though, does not view himself as an apostle and is uncomfortable with that type of talk. He said he is "a servant to others, to help whosoever that I can and give people encouragement and hope." Of course, many of those people that he tries to help are his fellow inmates, but his reach has also extended beyond prison. He is not permitted to use a computer and does not even know how to do so. However, friends have run various websites for him. His most recent website has a link for prayer requests, interview transcripts, and a message to young people who are involved in crime. Each day he works in the prison's mental health unit and serves as a peer counselor. Berkowitz views this work as part of his ministry.

As word got out about Berkowitz's conversion to Christianity, the media again came calling. He has become a Christian celebrity to the likes of Pat Robertson's "700 Club." Robertson said that Berkowitz is living proof that the devil is real and praised his newfound religion. Darrell Scott, whose daughter was killed in the Columbine High School shootings in Colorado, befriended Berkowitz after hearing about him through the fundamental Christian channels. Scott said that he read in Berkowitz's online journal that the story of his daughter inspired him, so Scott went to visit Berkowitz. "David

Berkowitz radiated the life of love of Jesus Christ," Scott said.

One of Berkowitz's most viewed interviews was the 1999 interview with Larry King. He told King, "...prison is not easy, but over the years, God has given me a lot of strength and a lot of hope to make it and to endure and to survive...he's done some miracles in my life, and he's brought me through a lot of things that maybe others would not have survived." Berkowitz is obviously uncomfortable discussing his past, saying it is too painful. He said to King, "I don't dwell on that much, and -- I don't dwell on it at all. It was a horrible thing. It was a horrible thing. It was the worst mistake of my life."

Even though Berkowitz does not like to talk about the murders he committed, he has not backed off of discussing crime, nor has the media stopped asking for his opinion. In an August 2012 interview, Berkowitz spoke about recent mass murders in America, including a shooting at a movie theater in Aurora, Colorado and another shooting at a temple in Wisconsin. He said that that society has glorified guns and that it needs to change. "I'm looking beyond gun control. That's for the legislators to wrangle with. My hope is just that young people would understand just how terrible this violence is. When they use a gun against someone else, they ruin their lives, too."

Berkowitz typically receives several letters a day. He gets up each morning at 5:30 a.m. and part of his daily routine is to sit down at his typewriter and type out his responses. In 2000, he wrote a letter of his own – to Neysa Moskowitz, Stacy's mother. After Berkowitz was arrested, Neysa told the media that she wanted Berkowitz dead, but New York did not have capital punishment when Berkowitz was arrested. Berkowitz reached out to her and apologized. The two actually developed a long-distance friendship, and he went so far as to send her Mother's Day cards. When a Christian sent him $20,000 out of admiration for his ministry, he sent $1,000 of it to Neysa. He did not keep any of it, he said, but wanted Neysa to have something. However, Neysa resumed her hatred for Berkowitz when he cancelled an in-person meeting in which he was going to give her information about her daughter's movie. The meeting was going to be filmed for television broadcast, but Berkowitz couldn't go through with it. He said, "It would be a circus. I had personal things to share I didn't want used."

News in 1998 that a movie was going to be made that featured the Son of Sam murders as part of its storyline also did not sit well with Berkowitz. Film director Spike Lee was 20 years old in the summer of 1977. It was a historic summer in New York, which was filled not just with stories about the Son of Sam, but a heat wave and the march of the New York Yankees to the World Series. Berkowitz was upset that Lee was, in his view dredging up the past with "Summer of Sam," saying that the only reason he was doing it was for money.

In 2000, a crime victim advocate from Houston sent a letter to 20 of the most notorious murderers in the United States. Andy Kahan asked the criminals, which included Charles Manson, Henry Lee Lucas, Richard Ramirez, and Berkowitz if they were aware that their letters and other personal belongings were being auctioned off for profit. The form letter also asked if they had personally profited from the sales. Those who profit from items related to murder are said to deal in "murderabilia." When Manson got the letter from Kahan, he sold it to a murderabilia dealer, who auctioned it on Ebay.

However, Berkowitz sent Kahan a letter that said he was bothered by this practice and that he would help Kahan any way he could. Berkowitz, whose personal effects command some of the highest prices on the market, also sent Kahan a notarized statement affirming that he does not sell his letters, autograph, or other belongings. This began a relationship between the two men in which they have collaborated on fighting the profiting from murderabilia. Berkowitz tips Kahan off if a dealer contacts him and Kahan said that it was Berkowitz's involvement that helped him convince Ebay to prohibit these types of auctions.

Carl Denaro is not especially impressed with Berkowitz's apparent change. He said of the attack, "I don't forgive him. I don't have a whole lot of hate and anger, possibly because

I'm still alive. That certainly has a lot to do with it. What he's doing now...he's a born-again Christian, which I think is just great, although when you're in prison for the rest of your life, I don't think there's a whole lot more to do."

There are many who are skeptical of his turn to Christianity in light of the heinous crimes Berkowitz has committed. His words and even his appearance are anything but menacing. His hair is gray, and he resembles someone's grandfather more than a mass murderer. He has publicly said that he does not think he should be allowed to leave prison. Parole hearings are required by the state of New York, despite his requests that they not occur. He said that part of the reason is that he is concerned about how the media will respond. He would rather that the families of his victims be allowed to get on with their lives. He wrote to George Pataki when Pataki was the governor of New York, "Frankly, I can give you no good reason why I should even be considered for parole. I can, however, give you many reasons why I should not be. The loss of six lives and the wounding of even more are reasons enough for the latter." Berkowitz has resigned himself to his fate and has created as much of a life for himself in prison as could be expected. Even if the motives for the crimes are still not entirely certain, Berkowitz seems fully aware of the torture that he put people through during his murder spree. "I continue to pray for the victims of my crimes. I do wish them the best in life. But I'm sure the pain will never end for them. I regret that."

REFERENCES

"CNN Larry King Weekend: Interview with David Berkowitz." CNN.com. http://transcripts.cnn.com/TRANSCRIPTS/0210/26/lklw.00.html

Connor, Tracy. "Breslin: Berkowitz Sticks to Me." New York Daily News, July 15, 2007. http://articles.sun-sentinel.com/2007-07-15/features/0707120426_1_jimmy-breslin-caliber-breslin-s-column

Fishman, Steve. "The Devil in David Berkowitz." New York. September 11, 2006.

Mahler, Jonathan. Ladies and Gentlemen, the Bronx is Burning. New York: Macmillan. 2006.

Philbin, Tom and Michael Philbin. The Killer Book of Serial Killers. Naperville, IL: Sourcebooks, Inc. 2008.

Rosen, Fred. There But for the Grace of God: Survivors of the 20th Century's Infamous Serial Killers. New York: Harper Collins. 2007.

Lightning Source UK Ltd.
Milton Keynes UK
UKHW020152291220
375862UK00009B/1751

9 781621 0746